Stegosaurus

Aaron Carr

MIGHTY DINOSAURS

AV2

www.av2books.com

Step 1
Go to **www.av2books.com**

Step 2
Enter this unique code

LGVKF7CMX

Step 3
Explore your interactive eBook!

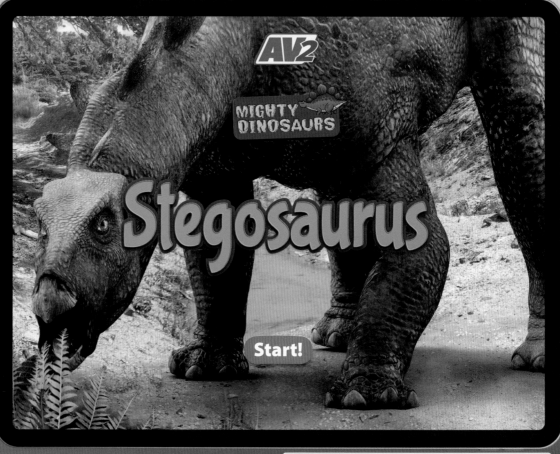

Start!

Your interactive eBook comes with...

Read

Audio
Listen to the entire book read aloud

Videos
Watch informative video clips

Weblinks
Gain additional information for research

Try This!
Complete activities and hands-on experiments

Key Words
Study vocabulary, and complete a matching word activity

Quizzes
Test your knowledge

Slideshows
View images and captions

View new titles and product videos at www.av2books.com

MIGHTY DINOSAURS

Stegosaurus

CONTENTS

Meet the Stegosaurus.

Its name means "roof lizard."

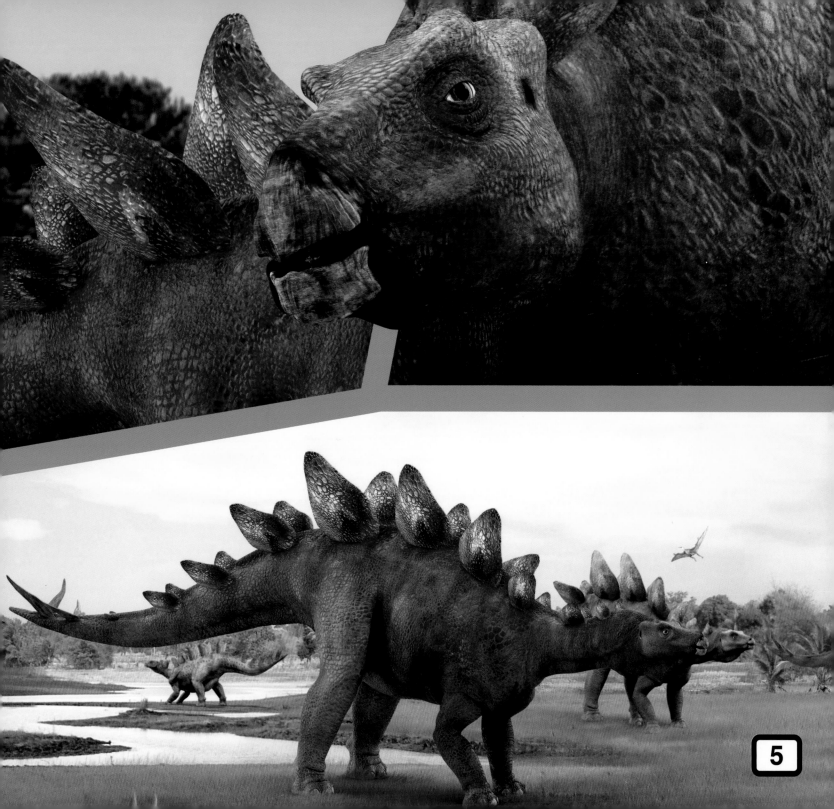

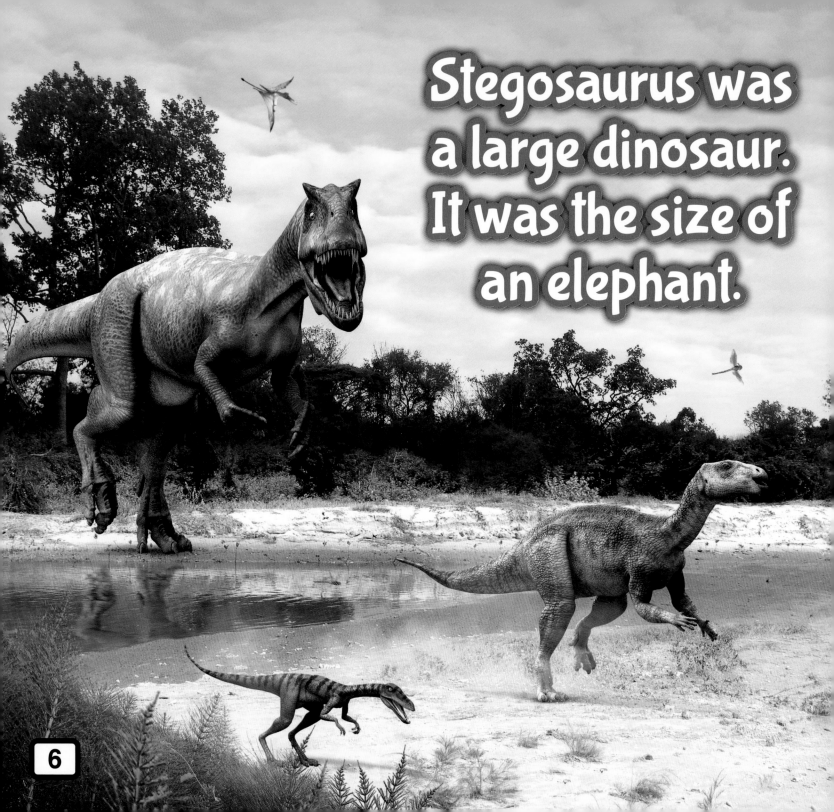

Stegosaurus was
a large dinosaur.
It was the size of
an elephant.

Stegosaurus had large, bony plates on its back.

It may have used these plates to keep itself safe.

Stegosaurus had 17 bony plates of different sizes.

9

Stegosaurus was a plant eater. It had a beak-shaped mouth that helped it tear its food.

Stegosaurus had a small head and a tiny brain. Its brain was about the size of a lime.

Stegosaurus moved slowly on four short legs.

Its top speed was only a little faster than a person can walk.

Stegosaurus lived in grasslands near lakes and rivers.

It lived in the west part of North America.

17

Stegosaurus died out about 150 million years ago.

Stegosaurus fossils formed over millions of years.

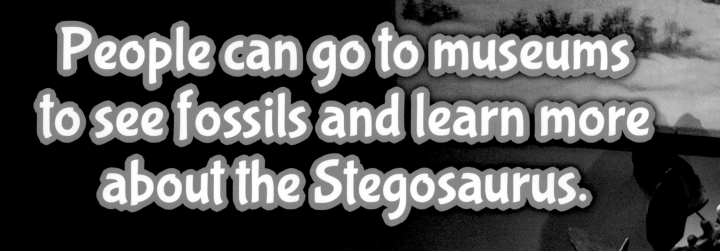

People can go to museums to see fossils and learn more about the Stegosaurus.

The Smithsonian National Museum of Natural History in Washington, D.C., has many Stegosaurus fossils.

Stegosaurus (steg-uh-SOR-us) is a thyreophoran dinosaur

Why did Stegosaurus have those bony plates on its back?

Stegosaurus Facts

These pages provide detailed information that expands on the interesting facts found in the book. They are intended to be used by adults as a learning support to help young readers round out their knowledge of each amazing dinosaur or pterosaur featured in the *Mighty Dinosaurs* series.

Pages 4–5

Stegosaurus means "roof lizard." The Stegosaurus is best known for its spiked tail and the bony plates along its back. Scientists once thought these plates lay flat along its back like a roof. The Stegosaurus's four-spiked tail is called a thagomizer. Scientists adopted this name after it was used in a 1982 cartoon called *Far Side*, which featured a group of cavemen talking about the Stegosaurus and its tail.

Pages 6–7

Stegosaurus was a large dinosaur. The Stegosaurus was a large, stocky dinosaur about the size of an elephant. It was more than 12 feet (3.7 meters) tall and about 30 feet (9 m) long. It could weigh as much as 3.4 tons (3 metric tons). This is about twice as heavy as a car.

Pages 8–9

Stegosaurus had large, bony plates on its back. The triangular plates were arranged in two rows running the length of the Stegosaurus's neck, back, and tail. The Stegosaurus had 17 bony plates all together. The plates were different sizes, but the largest could be up to 2.5 feet (0.8 m) in both height and length. Scientists used to think the plates were used for protection, but some scientists now believe they were only used to attract mates. Some scientists think the plates helped the Stegosaurus regulate its body temperature.

Pages 10–11

Stegosaurus was a plant eater, or herbivore. The Stegosaurus most likely ate mosses, cycads, ferns, horsetails, conifers, and fruits. It spent a large portion of each day searching for and eating food in order to sustain its large size. The Stegosaurus held its head near the ground for grazing. However, some scientists have suggested that the Stegosaurus may have been able to stand on its hind legs to browse for food from low tree branches.

Stegosaurus had a small head and a tiny brain. For such a large dinosaur, the Stegosaurus had a tiny head. Its head was even narrower than its neck. The Stegosaurus also had the smallest brain compared to its body size of all dinosaurs. Some scientists have even wondered if the Stegosaurus's lime-sized brain could control such a large body. They thought it must have had a second brain near its hips. However, this theory has since been disproved.

Stegosaurus could only move a little faster than a person can walk. The Stegosaurus had four short, powerful legs. Its hind legs were almost twice the length of its front legs. With its huge size and bulky body, the Stegosaurus was very slow. Scientists estimate that its top speed was about 3.7 miles (6 kilometers) per hour.

Stegosaurus lived in grasslands near lakes and rivers. Many Stegosauruses lived in what is now called the Morrison Formation, an expanse of rock that stretches from Montana to New Mexico. In this area, vast grassland plains with many rivers and lakes provided an ideal habitat for the Stegosaurus. The Stegosaurus is mostly thought to have lived in western North America, primarily in Utah, Colorado, and Wyoming. However, more recent discoveries have shown that the Stegosaurus also lived in what is now Portugal, Europe.

Stegosaurus lived about 150 million years ago during the Later Jurassic Period. Everything people know about the Stegosaurus comes from studying fossils. Fossils form when an animal dies and is covered in sand, mud, or water. This keeps the hard parts of the body, such as bones, teeth, and claws, from decomposing. The body is pressed between layers of mud and sand. Over millions of years, the layers turn into stone, and the dinosaur's bones and teeth turn into stone as well. This preserves the size and shape of the dinosaur.

People can go to museums to see fossils and learn more about the Stegosaurus. Each year, people from all over the world visit museums to see Stegosaurus fossils. The Smithsonian National Museum of Natural History in Washington, D.C., has fossils from several different species of Stegosaurus on display. The Smithsonian has one of the most complete fossils of a Stegosaurus ever found.

KEY WORDS

Research has shown that as much as 65 percent of all written material published in English is made up of 300 words. These 300 words cannot be taught using pictures or learned by sounding them out. They must be recognized by sight. This book contains 46 common sight words to help young readers improve their reading fluency and comprehension. This book also teaches young readers several important content words, such as proper nouns. These words are paired with pictures to aid in learning and improve understanding.

Page	Sight Words First Appearance	Page	Content Words First Appearance
4	its, means, name, the	4	lizard, Stegosaurus
6	a, an, it, large, of, was	6	dinosaur, elephant, size
8	back, different, had, have, keep, may, on, these, to	8	plates
10	food, plant, that	10	eater, mouth
12	about, and, head, small	12	brain, lime
14	four	14	legs
15	can, little, only, than, walk	15	person, speed
16	in, near, rivers	16	grasslands, lakes
17	part	17	North America
18	out, years	19	fossils
19	over	20	museums, Smithsonian National Museum of Natural History, Washington, D.C.
20	go, has, learn, many, more, people, see		

Published by AV2
350 5th Avenue, 59th Floor
New York, NY 10118
Website: www.av2books.com

Library of Congress Control Number: 2019950232

ISBN 978-1-7911-1664-4 (hardcover)
ISBN 978-1-7911-1665-1 (softcover)
ISBN 978-1-7911-1666-8 (multi-user eBook)

Printed in Guangzhou, China
1 2 3 4 5 6 7 8 9 0 24 23 22 21 20

022020
100919

Project Coordinator: Priyanka Das
Art Director: Terry Paulhus

Every reasonable effort has been made to trace ownership and to obtain permission to reprint copyright material. The publishers would be pleased to have any errors or omissions brought to their attention so that they may be corrected in subsequent printings.

All illustrations by Jon Hughes, pixel-shack.com. AV2 acknowledges Getty and Shutterstock as its primary image suppliers for this title.